Plants of Wax

Laurence Vail Coleman

ISBN 978-1-300-26456-9
90000
9 781300 264569

AMERICAN MUSEUM OF NATURAL HISTORY

PLANTS OF WAX

By LAURENCE VAIL COLEMAN, M.A.

GUIDE LEAFLET SERIES, No. 54 FEBRUARY, 1922

AMERICAN·MUSEUM·PRESS

HACKENSACK MEADOW GROUP

Showing a great variety of foliage

A PORTION OF THE BULLFROG GROUP
Showing Pickerel Weed

Plants of Wax

How They are Made in The American Museum of Natural History

By Laurence Vail Coleman, M.A.

Plants of wax have become familiar to museum goers chiefly in connection with habitat groups of mammals, birds and reptiles. In fact, the impressiveness of a group often depends as much upon the accessories which enter into its composition as upon the specimens which it features, and therefore the making of artificial foliage has become an important branch of work in a museum's studios.

The following account explains how plants are made in the American Museum. The method employed for leaves was devised and patented by Carl E. Akeley, and this brief exposition is published with his consent.

The principal materials required are bleached beeswax, cotton batting of good quality, annealed and stiff iron wire of various sizes, and a few tools, such as are shown in the cut. Fingers must do the rest; tools will not give mechanical ability any more than brushes and colors will make an artist. For delicate leaves, or the petals of flowers, mousseline de soie, the mysterious "fabric" of the Mintorns, is needed. This was formerly used in making leaves, but has given way to the more practical and economical method of Akeley. The agate burnisher, a tool used by gilders, is rather a luxury and a home-made tool of brass or iron will serve the purpose. The use of this is to smooth down rough spots,

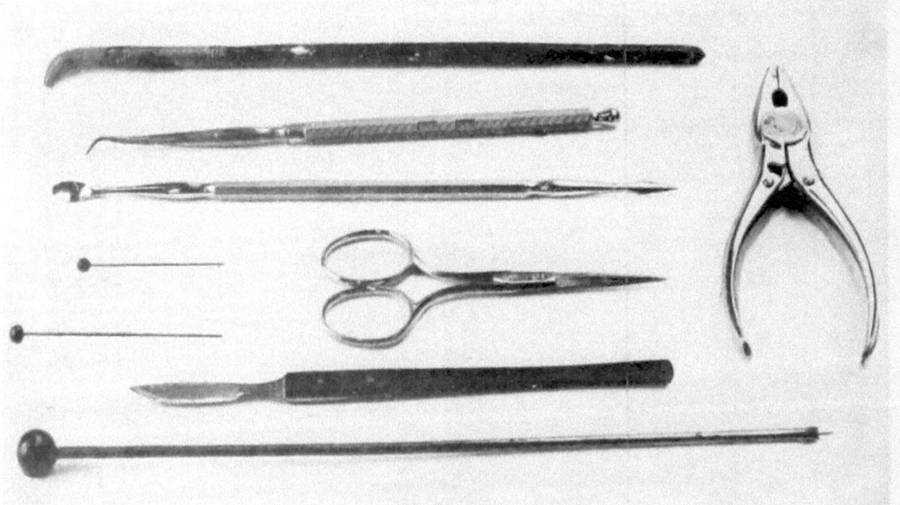

TOOLS USED IN MAKING LEAVES AND FLOWERS OF WAX

or points, and to weld together leaves like those of the pitcher plant that are made in two or more parts.

Do not be discouraged if your first efforts are not successful, or not as successful as you expected. Printed directions can give you only general principles; something depends on natural aptitude, much on care and patience. Try something easy first.

WAX LEAVES

In making artificial foliage the individual leaf is the preparator's first concern. A fresh leaf makes the best model, though one preserved

in a bath of formalin and glycerine[1] may be used. By word and picture let us follow the reproduction of a leaf.

MAKING A SQUEEZE MOLD

The original leaf is placed upon a bed of clay around which a clay wall is set up and the enclosure so formed is poured full of plaster

THE LEAF, RESTING ON A CLAY BED
Ready for Making the First Half of the Mold

[1]A mixture of formalin 15 parts, water 35 parts and glycerine 50 parts is best for prolonged preservation of foliage. Leaves immersed in a stronger mixture for a few days and then removed and dried will usually retain their form and if so treated may be recolored and used for exhibition, but the result is seldom satisfactory.

which covers one side of the leaf and soon sets. The clay is then removed, leaving the leaf and the plaster together. Two notches or keys are cut in opposite edges of the plaster to receive the keys of the second part of the mold and to prevent the two parts slipping on one another. The margin around the leaf is brushed with clay water or soap solution to

THE LEAF, RESTING ON THE FIRST HALF OF THE MOLD
Ready for Making the Second Half

prevent the next layer of plaster from adhering to it, and for best results the soap is then swabbed off and a film of stearin applied; another wall is set up around the leaf and its plaster bed and into the little basin thus

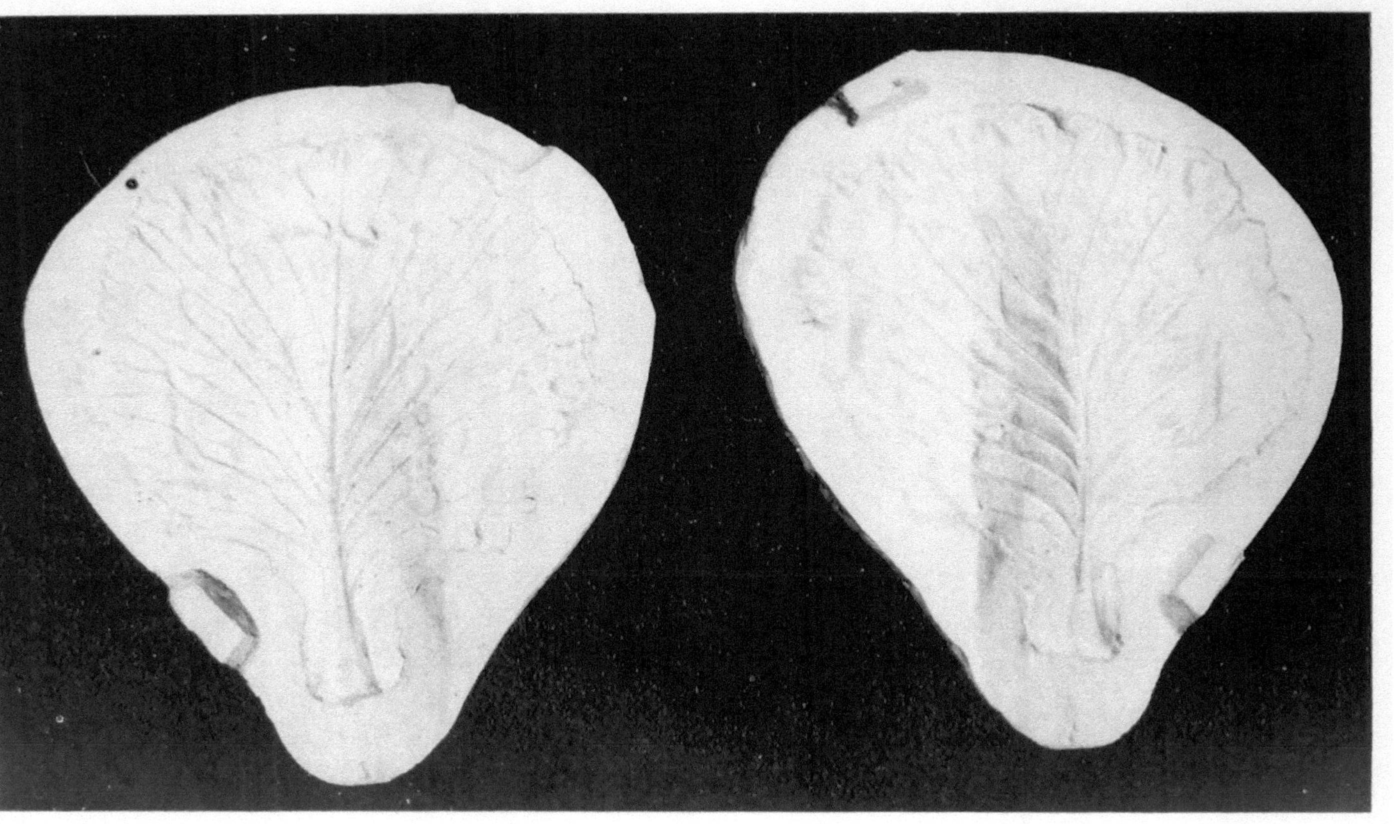

THE TWO HALVES OF A SIMPLE MOLD

formed is poured plaster which covers the second side of the leaf. When it sets, the two blocks of plaster may be separated and the leaf between them will have left its impression on the inner face of each. It will be seen that each key on the first block has now its mate on the second, for tongues of plaster from the last-poured mass have filled the notches cut in the first one. Thus the two parts interlock and fit together in one position only.

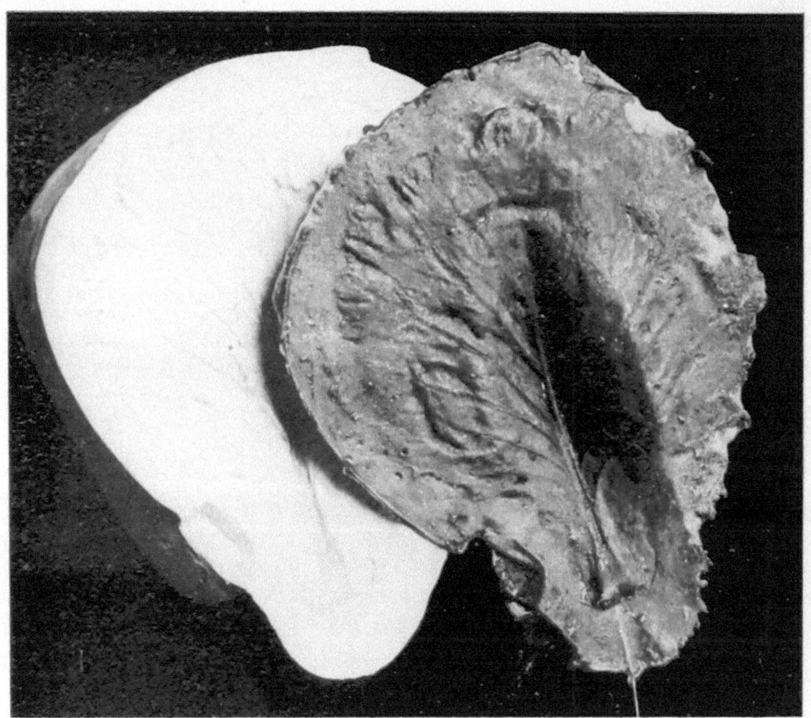

THE WAX LEAF READY FOR TRIMMING

The mold is now set aside to dry and before using hardened by boiling in a strong solution of borax for about twenty minutes or soaking in melted paraffin for about the same time. Molds treated with paraffin give the best impression but are a little difficult to use on account of the tendency of the wax to stick to them. In case a mold is going to be used a great many times, it is best to soak it in linseed oil for five minutes and let it dry for a week or two.

CASTING A WAX LEAF

When leaves are to be cast from a squeeze mold, the mold must be soaked in hot water and used while warm and moist. Heat keeps the wax from chilling till it fills the mold and moisture prevents it from adhering to the plaster. A film of cotton is laid upon one side of the mold—better the concave side if either one is so. A piece of cotton-covered hard iron wire[1] is laid along the line of the midrib, with its end projecting

THREE STAGES IN TRIMMING A VERY SIMPLE LEAF

to form a stem, and if the leaf be a thick one more cotton is laid on top. Melted wax, tinted green with oil colors, is then poured upon the cotton and the upper part of the mold squeezed down upon it. The whole is plunged into cold water, opened and the cast removed.

The wax should be bleached beeswax to which should be added about a tablespoonful of Canada balsam to each quart of melted wax, the object of the balsam being to toughen the wax. Wax should be

[1]For small leaves the cotton covered millinery wire of commerce is employed, but for larger ones it is desirable to use iron wire of a larger size. The wire is tapered with a file or on an emery wheel and then wrapped with cotton by twirling it through the fingers.

melted in a double boiler, such as is used for cooking oatmeal in order to avoid burning the wax and to lessen the danger from fire.

A HEAVY COMPLEX LEAF
Showing the Wire Supports on the Under Side

The oil color is thinned with a very little turpentine and thoroughly stirred into the melted wax; this gives the body color of the leaf to be imitated.

It will be found that pressure aided by capillarity has forced the wax into a thin sheet which has engulfed the cotton and the wire so

that neither can be seen, and that the excess of wax has run out around the leaf. The manipulations of casting may be performed in a few seconds.

Much time is saved by using three molds in rotation so that while one is in use a second may be warming in hot water and a third with its cast may be cooling in the cold bath.

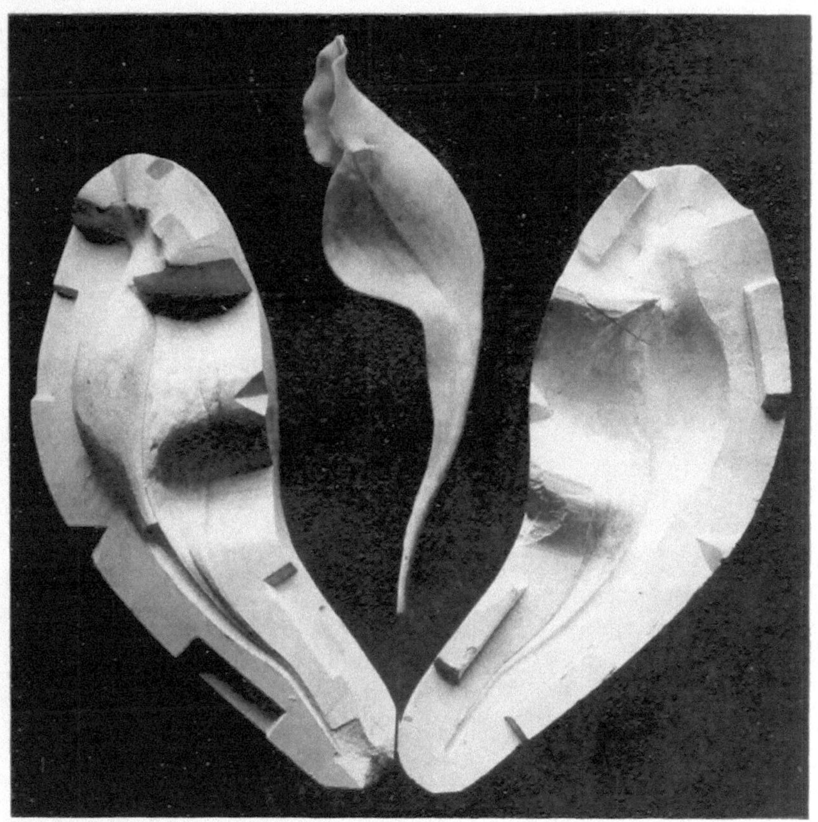

A COMPLETE LEAF OF THE PITCHER PLANT
And the Molds Used in Making One-Half of It

A Pair of Molds is Needed for Each Half of the Leaf, the Keel, Shown in the Picture Being Made on One of the Halves

In the case of large, heavy, and, especially, deeply scalloped leaves such as occur on many tropical plants, it is necessary to make a somewhat elaborate complicated framework, such as is indicated in the figure,

by twisting together a number of wires so that one underlies each arm or part of the leaf. These wires are wound with cotton batting or gauze, tapering from their junction with the midrib to the tip.

In making these large leaves, it is often advantageous for two persons to busy themselves with a single mold, one person pouring the wax and the other manipulating the mold and removing the casts. For large parti-colored leaves two colors of wax, perhaps green and red, may be poured into the same mold.

METAL SQUEEZE MOLDS

A mold is sometimes attached to a large hinge or frame by means of which it may be opened or closed after the fashion of a lemon-squeezer. Metal molds— half type metal and half bronze—may be employed if a large number of leaves is required, and such a mold must always be attached to a hinged frame.

FINISHING A WAX LEAF

The cast as it is taken from the mold must first be trimmed. Scissors are usually employed but the operation is not a simple one if the edge of the leaf be serrate. In this event, the scissors, which have been warmed, are jerked along, alternately cutting ahead and edging to the side. Then with a warm tool imperfections are removed, and finally the leaf is shaped between the fingers.

The wire which projects from the base of the leaf is wrapped with a strip of mousseline-de-soie (a gauze of the utmost delicacy) dipped in wax. Once more the tool is applied to the stem to obliterate all traces of successive windings and the leaf is finished save for a final coloring.

The manner of assembling leaves upon their stems is determined by the habit of the plant, the manner in which the leaves are arranged around the main stem. The leaves of herbs are lashed with thread to a wire of proper size to represent the main shaft of the plant, and the joints are wrapped with gauze, the windings being continued along the shaft. Stiff iron wire should be used for this purpose, and to insure a neat piece of work the end filed to a long taper. Leaves of trees are usually treated in the same way, only the tender twigs being reproduced, for the larger woody twigs need not be fabricated, but in their natural state serve as a base to which the wax tips are attached.

In fastening leaves to the woody twigs, a hole is bored diagonally through the twig with a fine drill, if you are fortunate enough to have one, or with a triangular glover's needle held in a pin vise or set in a little wooden handle. The leaf wire is passed through the hole, bent down along the twig, and wrapped with gauze. In the absence of gauze, thin, tough brown paper, cut in narrow strips, will do fairly well.

When the work of assembling has been done, the final touches of color are applied. A large air-brush which delivers a spray of oil color thinned in turpentine is really a necessity where leaves are to be made in considerable numbers; where only a few are wanted color may be stippled on with a brush or wad of cotton batting and good results may often be obtained by rubbing in dry color.

Frequently ten thousand leaves are needed for a single group, but it is rarely necessaryto make more than half a dozen sizes of one kind, so hundreds of leaves may be cast from a single mold.

Blades of grass are cut from heavily waxed gauze and are modeled by folding them lengthwise over the edge of a knifelike strip of tin fixed in a wooden base. Very little manipulation is required. No rib is used,

but each blade from a short distance above the base is rolled about a wire and several blades are then attached to a heavier wire stem.

In making cactus, the spines are removed and a piece mold made of the plant or of the various branches. In the case of such a form as the barrel cactus, the body is often made hollow to save wax and while still in the mold, backed with a lining of plaster and burlap.

WAX FLOWERS

Success in making artificial flowers depends largely upon ingenuity

A SPRAY OF DOGWOOD
A Very Simple Flower

in the application of a few general principles, though to make small flowers on an extensive scale necessitates the use of dies, such as are shown in the cut and unfortunately, the making of dies calls for the services of an expert machinist. Large or medium-sized flowers, poppies, for example, can be made without any special appliances.

The first step is always to dismember the natural flower in order to determine its construction, and ordinarily it will be found to consist of a central bulb-like pistil surrounded by slender stamens, a set of petals

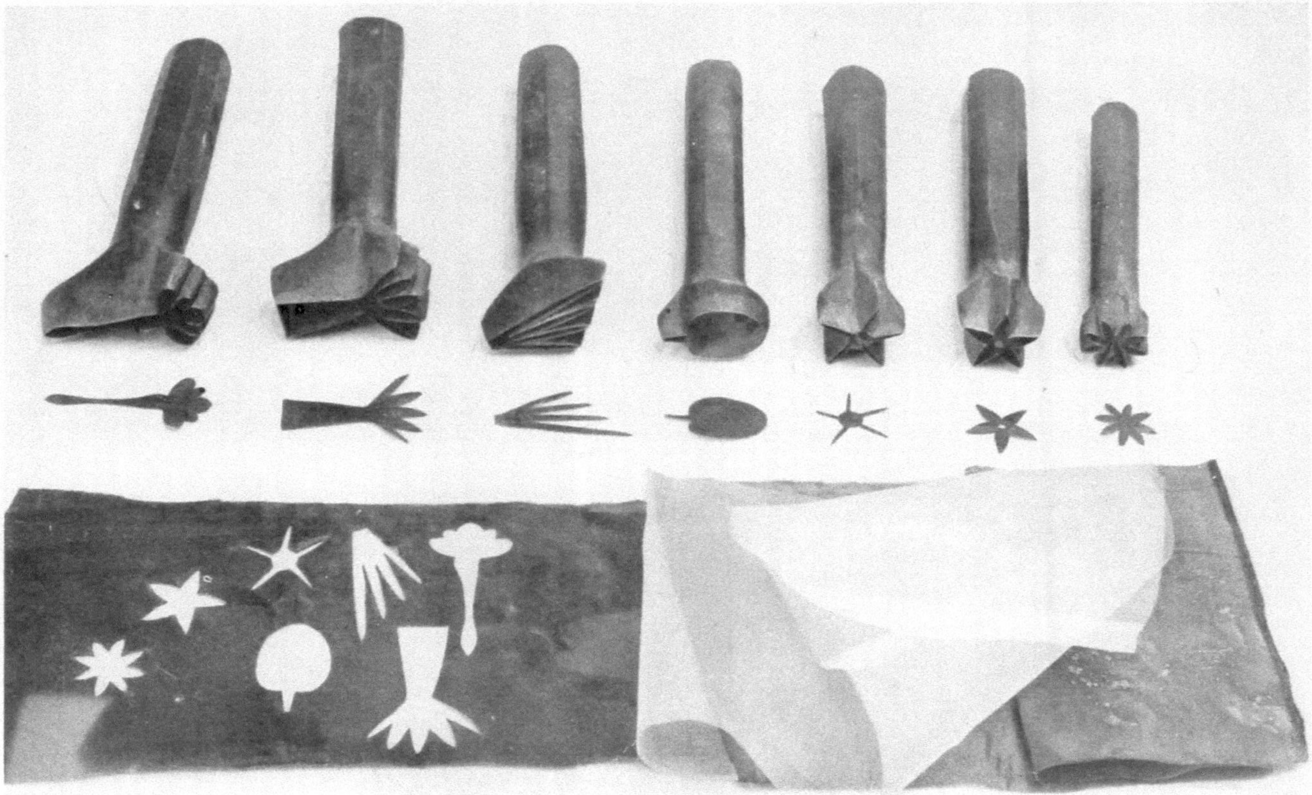

DIES USED IN MAKING FLOWERS

collectively termed the corolla framing this heart and a calyx covering the junction of the flower with the stem.

When the pistil is large enough to be of any consequence it is cast upon the end of a wire which is later wound with waxed gauze to the size of the stem. The stamens are usually long filaments, each bearing a nodule or anther at its tip, and they are usually imitated with waxed threads or wires of which the tips are dipped in wax. To imitate stamens which are short, stout and numerous, it may be practicable to fray or lacerate one edge of a strip of waxed gauze and so to make a sort of limp comb which may be wound around the stem with the points upstanding.

The conspicuous and often highly colored corolla is either a group of separate petals or a cup formed by their fusion. The daisy and the morning-glory illustrate respectively these two conditions. Separated petals, if small, are usually cut or stamped with a metal die from waxed gauze, and for convenience they may sometimes be made in one piece, joined together at the bases. Large petals are usually cast just as if they were leaves on a basis of gauze, or, if large, cotton batting, and are then welded to the stem one at a time. A "one-piece" corolla is split down one side and laid out flat as a pattern for cutting, stamping or casting similar pieces. Each artificial corolla is then curled around the stem like a cone and the two adjoining edges are welded together with a hot tool.

The basal calyx frequently has the form of a star, which may be punched out and the stem slipped through a hole in its center, but sometimes it is composed a large petal-like parts which must be made separately and attached to the stem.

The ground color of all parts is mixed into the wax of which they are made, and the finishing tints are applied by hand or with an air-brush which delivers liquid color as a spray.

www.ingramcontent.com/pod-product-compliance
Ingram Content Group UK Ltd.
Pitfield, Milton Keynes, MK11 3LW, UK
UKHW041902190726
13854UKWH00003B/1044

9 781300 264569